Easter Activities

Fiona Watt and Ray Gibson

Designed by Sarah Sherley-Price, Andrea Slane and Jo Webb

Photographs by Howard Allman

Illustrated by Amanda Barlow, Chris Chaisty, Michaela Kennard,
Sarah Sherley-Price, Nelupa Hussain and Andrea Slane

Additional photography: Ray Moller

Contents

Pecking hens and chicks

1. Fold a paper plate in half. Crease the fold well. Then, paint the back of the plate.

2. Fold the plate in half, again. For a beak, cut a triangle from paper and glue it on.

3. Cut some triangles from bright paper. These are the spikes on top of the head.

Cut feather shapes from paper and glue them on.

For a chick, put a saucer on stiff paper and cut it out. Don't add the spikes to the head.

Tape the tail onto the back of the plate.

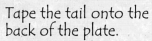

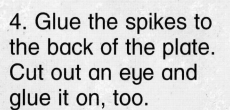

4. Glue the spikes to the back of the plate. Cut out an eye and glue it on, too.

5. Cut lots of thin strips of bright tissue paper. Make them as long as your hand.

6. Put the strips into a bunch and twist them together at one end. Tape them on for a tail.

Rock the hens and chicks to make them peck.

Bunny wrapping paper

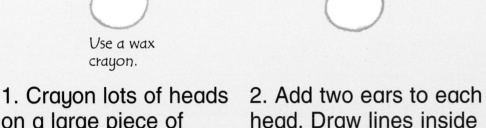

Use a wax crayon.

1. Crayon lots of heads on a large piece of paper. Space them out.

2. Add two ears to each head. Draw lines inside the ears, too.

3. Use the same crayon to draw a fat body below each head.

4. Draw two feet below the bunny's body, and a wavy line for a tail.

5. Add eyes, a nose and a curved mouth to each bunny.

6. Add whiskers. Then fill in the bunnies with felt-tip pens.

You could try drawing a bunny like this, too.

Wrap Easter presents in your decorated paper.

For a gift tag, draw a bunny, then cut around it and glue it onto a piece of stiff paper.

Field of rabbits

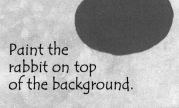

Paint the rabbit on top of the background.

1. Press your hand into yellow paint, then press it all over a piece of paper. Add green on top.

2. When the paint is dry, dip a finger into some paint and finger paint a fat shape.

3. For a head, dip your finger in the paint again and rub your finger around and around.

4. Dip a finger into the paint again and add ears. Add four legs on the rabbit's body.

5. Dip a fingertip into white paint and add a tail. Add tiny dots for eyes, too.

6. When the paint is dry, use a felt-tip pen to add a nose, a dot in the eye and whiskers.

You could print flowers around the rabbits with a fingertip.

Decorated eggs

Dyed eggs

1. Hard boil an egg. Let it cool. Draw patterns on it with a wax crayon.

2. Pour bright food dye into the bottom of a small bowl.

3. Put the egg into the bowl. Dab the food dye all over it with a brush.

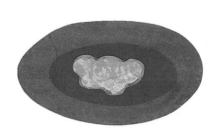

4. Lift the egg out with a spoon. Put it on some paper towels to dry.

5. Pour a little cooking oil onto a saucer or into a shallow dish.

This makes the egg shiny.

6. Dip a paper towel in the oil and rub it all over the egg.

Patterned eggs

1. Hard boil an egg. Let it cool and dry it well on a paper towel.

2. Cut small pieces of masking tape and press them all over.

Try drawing stripes around the egg with different pens.

For stars like these, overlap strips of tape.

3. Use fat felt-tip pens to draw patches all over the egg.

4. When the patches have dried, peel off the tape to leave a pattern.

These patterns are better if you decorate white or light brown eggs.

A chick card

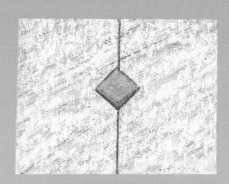

1. Cut the corner off an old envelope. Crayon all over one side of it, and inside, too.

2. Fold a piece of stiff paper in half. Crease the fold well, then open it out again.

3. Glue the corner of the envelope in the middle of the card. This makes the beak.

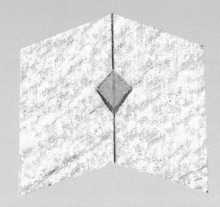

You could cut out half an egg shape and glue it on below your chick.

4. Lift the top of the beak. Close the card and rub across it to flatten the beak.

5. Open the card. Draw a chick around the beak. Add some eyes, legs and feet.

Paint streaks across some paper with a big brush. Glue on a beak when the paint is dry.

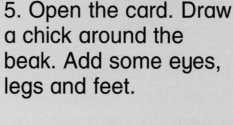

6. Draw flowers around the chick, or cut them out from bright paper and glue them on.

For a long card, glue body shapes over the fold, then add the beaks.

Try gluing on little pieces of tissue paper for a body.

Sheep and lambs picture

You don't need to wind it neatly.

1. For the bodies, draw big and little wavy shapes, like these, on pieces of thin paper. Then, cut them out.

2. Dip the shapes into water. Shake off the drops, then arrange them on a large piece of paper.

3. Tape the end of some wool or yarn onto an old birthday card or postcard. Wind the yarn around and around.

Make sure both pieces of tape are on the same side.

4. When the card is covered, cut off any leftover yarn. Secure the end of the yarn with a piece of tape.

5. Paint the yarn green on the side without the tape. Press it all over the paper. Add more paint as you go.

6. Gently peel off the paper bodies. When the paint is dry, add faces and legs with paint or a thick felt-tip pen.

Use a fingertip to print flowers in the grass.

A chick puppet

1. Fold three paper plates in half. Then, fold each one back the other way, along each fold.

You don't need these pieces.

2. Cut one of the plates in half along its fold. Cut a strip from the edge of one half.

Try rolling two different shades of crêpe paper together, then cut the slits (see step 7).

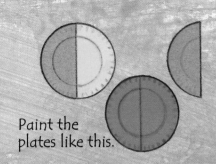

Paint the plates like this.

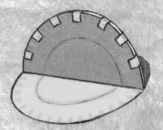

3. Mix some household (PVA) glue with yellow, red and orange paints. Paint the plates.

4. When the paint is dry, fold the two whole plates and put them together, like this.

5. Carefully join the orange and red parts together with lots of small pieces of tape.

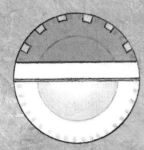

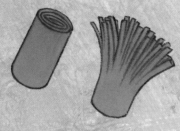

6. Turn the plates over and tape the smaller orange piece of plate onto the red half.

7. Cut a strip of crêpe paper as long as your hand. Roll it tightly, then cut lots of slits.

8. Tape the crêpe paper roll to the back of the yellow part. Tape it on near the top.

9. Cut eyes from paper and glue them on. Cut middles for the eyes and glue them on, too.

10. Cut a hole in a sock. Put your hand into the sock and push your thumb through the hole.

11. Put your hand into the bird, like this. Open and close your hand to make the bird talk.

Rabbit face

To make rabbit 'ears', tie your hair in bunches and use hair gel to make them stand up.

1. Rub a damp sponge into some lilac face paint. Rub it lightly around and around.

2. Dab the sponge onto one cheek and twist it a little. Lift your hand and dab it on again.

Put on a matching T-shirt before you paint your face.

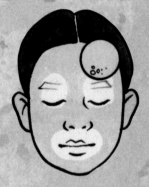

If you don't have lilac face paint, you can mix other paints to make it (see below).

3. Dab the face paint over the cheeks, nose and chin. Leave a bare patch around the mouth.

4. Continue dabbing paint onto the forehead, leaving bare patches around the eyes.

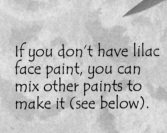

5. With closed eyes and mouth, dab white face paint onto the bare patches.

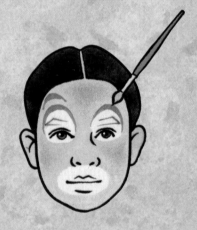

6. Sponge darker lilac on the cheeks and forehead. Brush on pink eyebrows.

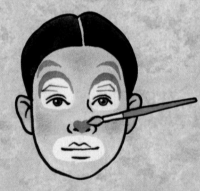

7. Dip the brush in the pink face paint again and paint the tip of the nose, like this.

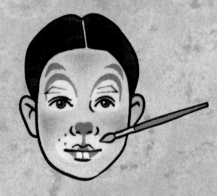

8. Paint a line from the nose to the top lip. Fill in the bottom lip. Add dots, whiskers and teeth.

Mixing paints

If you don't have lilac face paint, you can make it by mixing together red, white and blue paints.

Mix them to make purple.

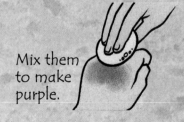

1. Dab red face paint on the back of your hand. Add some blue.

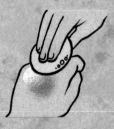

2. Clean your sponge then dab on a little white to make lilac.

Potato-printed chicks

1. Lay several kitchen paper towels onto a thick pile of old newspapers.

2. Pour some bright yellow paint on top. Spread the paint with the back of a spoon.

3. Cut a potato in half. Then, cut away the two sides, like this, to make a handle.

4. Dip the cut side of the potato into the paint then press it firmly onto some paper.

5. Cut a triangle from bright orange or red paper and glue it onto the side of the body.

6. When the paint is dry, add an eye, wings, a tail and some feet with a black felt-tip pen.

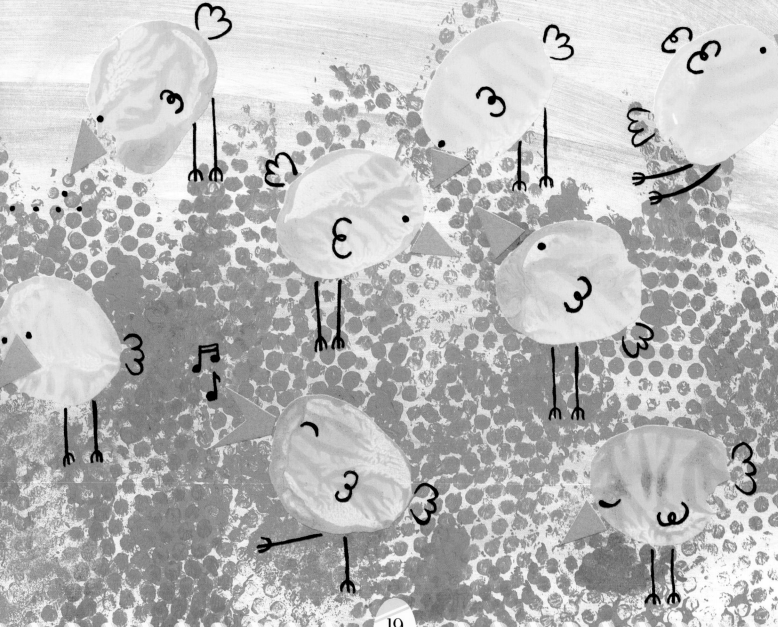

Giant spring flower prints

Primroses

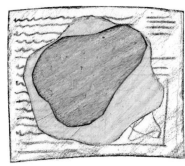

1. Spread yellow paint onto a newspaper. Cut a small, hard pear in half and press it into the paint.

2. Press the pear onto some paper, then lift it off. Put a bottle top at the pointed end of the shape you have printed.

3. Print more pear shapes around the bottle top. Dip the pear in the paint each time you do a print.

The prints on these pages are much smaller than the ones you will do.

4. Lift off the bottle top. Then, dip a finger tip into green paint. Print dots in the middle of the pear prints.

5. For big leaves, cut a large potato in half. Dip it in green paint and press it onto the paper, around the flower.

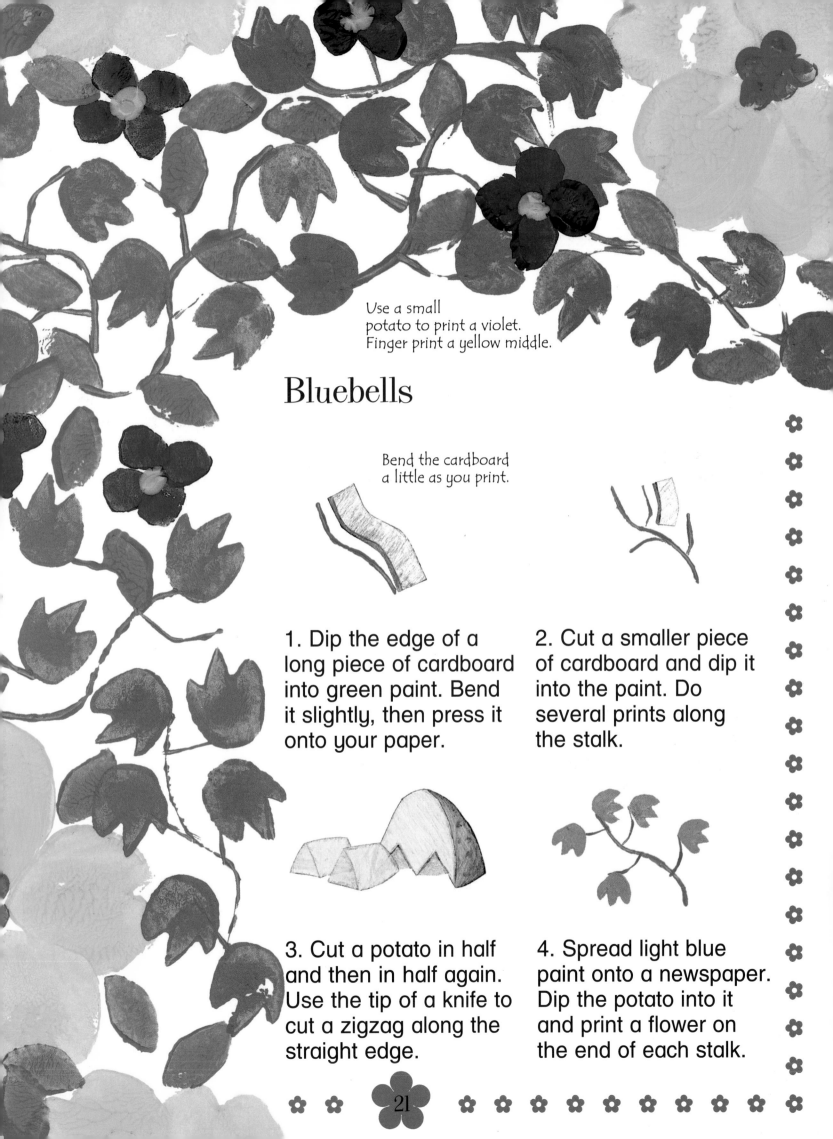

Use a small
potato to print a violet.
Finger print a yellow middle.

Bluebells

Bend the cardboard
a little as you print.

1. Dip the edge of a long piece of cardboard into green paint. Bend it slightly, then press it onto your paper.

2. Cut a smaller piece of cardboard and dip it into the paint. Do several prints along the stalk.

3. Cut a potato in half and then in half again. Use the tip of a knife to cut a zigzag along the straight edge.

4. Spread light blue paint onto a newspaper. Dip the potato into it and print a flower on the end of each stalk.

Bunny napkin rings

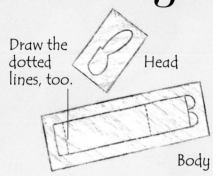

Draw the dotted lines, too.

Head

Body

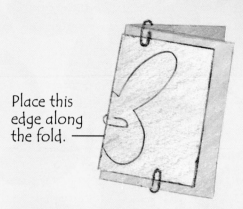

Place this edge along the fold.

1. Cut a piece of greaseproof paper the size of this page. Use paperclips to secure it over page 23.

2. Draw around the templates of the head and body. Then, cut the templates apart, like this.

3. Fold a piece of stiff paper in half. Then, use paperclips to clip the template of the head to the paper, like this.

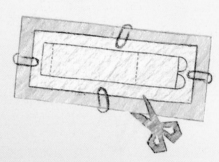

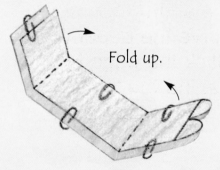

Fold up.

4. Carefully cut around the shape of the head. Then, open out the paper and use felt-tip pens to draw a face.

5. Clip the template of the body onto some stiff paper and cut it out. Then, clip the template back onto it.

6. Fold the paper along the dotted lines on the template. Crease the folds well, then remove the template.

Glue along here.

Remember to trace the dotted lines on the template.

7. Put some glue along the short edge, then curve the paper over. Stick the edge just behind the feet.

8. Turn the head over and put two blobs of glue under the ears. Press the head onto the body.

Roll up a napkin and push it through the bunny.

To bend a bunny's ear, roll it around a pencil.

9. To make a tail, pull a little piece off a cotton ball. Roll it into a ball, then glue it on the back of the body.

Surprise eggs

1. Trim any rough edges from around a cardboard egg carton. Paint the inside with a bright paint.

2. Turn the carton upside-down and paint the outside with the same paint. Leave the box to dry.

3. Tap the pointed end of an egg with a spoon, to crack the shell. Pull off the pieces of broken shell and tip out the egg.

4. Wash the empty shell under cold water, then leave it upside-down to dry. Crack and clean five more eggs.

5. Use crayons and food dye to decorate the eggshells. (The steps on page 8 show you how to do this.)

6. Put a tiny Easter gift, such as a small Easter egg or a toy, inside each eggshell. Put the eggs into the carton.

7. To decorate the box, fold pieces of bright

8. Close the egg box and tie a ribbon

You could hide small chocolate Easter eggs inside the eggs.

Cut flowers from wrapping paper and glue them on.

Use a felt-tip pen to add antennae to the butterflies.

You could finger print flowers all over the carton.

Glue sequins onto the carton if you like.

A bunch of daffodils

1. Draw a 12x12cm (5x5in.) square of bright yellow crêpe paper. Cut it out, then cut the square in half.

Tie a ribbon around the straws.

2. Make a frill all along one edge by stretching the crêpe paper gently between your fingers and thumbs.

3. Wrap the paper around the end of a wooden spoon. Slide it off a little and twist it into a point.

Snip each petal here.

4. Fold the other piece of paper in half, short sides together. Fold it in half, then in half again. Cut it into a petal shape.

5. Open out the petals, then snip off two of the petals. Snip between each petal to separate them a little more.

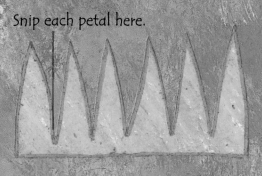

6. Wrap the petals around the paper on the spoon. Wet your thumb and finger and twist the end into a point, again.

Cut out leaves from green paper.

Snip here.

7. Cut a piece off a straw, half-way down the short end. Snip the end to make two slits, like this.

8. Pull the paper off the spoon and dip the twisted end into glue. Push it into the straw and leave it to dry.

Use white crêpe paper to make narcissi. Draw along the frilled edge with an orange felt-tip pen.

9. Gently pull down each petal. Pull them a little so that they fan out evenly around the middle piece.

For a bouquet, wrap the ends of the straws in some tissue paper.

Easter flowerpots

Add more strips if there is room.

1. Cut two strips of masking tape and press them on either side of a terracotta pot.

2. Cut two more strips and press them onto the pot. Press the ends inside the pot, like this.

3. Cut more strips of masking tape and press them in between the other strips.

Scrunch up the paper towel.

You can wash the paint off the eraser, later.

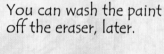

4. Put a little acrylic paint onto a saucer. Dip a paper towel into it and dab it between the strips.

5. Fill in between all the strips of tape. Let the paint dry, then peel off the tape.

6. Put a different paint onto the saucer, then dip an eraser on the end of a pencil into it.

Cut out flowers from wrapping paper and glue them on.

Chicken and egg card

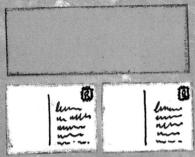  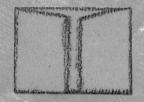

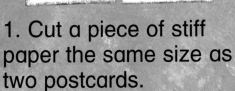

1. Cut a piece of stiff paper the same size as two postcards.

2. Fold the paper in half, short sides together. Open it out.

3. Fold the short sides in, so that they meet at the middle fold.

Make the egg slightly smaller than the card.

Glue the egg across the middle of the card.

Don't cut the back of the card.

4. Draw an egg on the back of some wrapping paper, then cut it out.

5. Glue the egg on the card. Draw a zigzag from top to bottom.

6. Pull the front and back apart and cut along the zigzag.

Decorate the inside of the card with flowers.

For an Easter present, you could plant some spring flowers in your pot.

7. Press the eraser onto the pot to make the five petals of a flower, like this.

8. Wash the eraser, then dip it into a different shade. Add a middle to each flower.

7. Draw a chick on yellow paper. Cut it out. Add eyes and a beak.

8. Glue the chick over the fold in the middle of the card.

9. Draw legs with a felt-tip pen. Decorate the inside of the card.

Use bright wrapping paper with a small pattern.

Cress egg-heads

1. Follow steps 3 and 4 on page 24 to crack the top off an egg. Fill it with cotton balls.

2. Use a spoon to pour in water. Tip the egg so that any excess water drains out.

Overlap the ends.

3. Put the egg into an egg carton. Sprinkle it with half a teaspoon of cress or mustard seeds.

4. Put the egg in a light place. Add a little water every day. The cress will grow in 7-8 days.

5. Cut a narrow strip from the short side of postcard. Bend it around and tape it.

Add a beak and wings for a chick.

6. Stand the egg on top of the cardboard. Add a face with felt-tip pens and paper.

Cut out ears and glue them on for an Easter bunny.